BELIEVE & RISE

The Power of Your Story
How to create an
Empowering Belief

EMMANUEL SANGALANG

Emmanuel Sangalang

Believe & Rise

Copyright © 2021 Emmanuel Sangalang
All rights reserved.
ISBN: 9798786652728
Imprint: Independently published

Emmanuel Sangalang

DEDICATION

First off. I would like to dedicate this book to my children Kaleiya, Ethan, Eva and Kyver. This book is a prime example to go after your dreams. Your hard work will always pay off.

To my Mastermind Guys. All of you have played a major part into the creation of this book. I appreciate all of you! Ho Yah!

My family & friends who shown me nothing but love. Thank you!

Lastly, my wife KC. I dedicate this book to you. Thank you for your endless support and constant reminder to always be myself. None of this would be possible if it wasn't for you. All of our life's challenges continues to make us stronger. I love you and thank you so much!

Emmanuel Sangalang

Table of Contents

Introduction — 9

Chapter 1 — 14
Beware of Your Labels
(Reminisce, Label Exercise)

Chapter 2 — 23
Definitions, Emotions
(Defining Labels, Emotional Triggers)

Chapter 3 — 36
Body Language (Movement Exercise)

Chapter 4 — 42
Breaking the Pattern (Pattern Exercise)

Chapter 5 — 47
What & Why? (3 Categories)

Chapter 6 — 67
Power Stance (Your Move)

Chapter 7 — 72
Exciting Emotions (Expressing Energy)

Chapter 8 — 76
Permission (Implementation Exercise)

Chapter 9 — 80
Identity (New Identity)

Chapter 10 — 85
Empowering Belief (Mirror Exercise)

Emmanuel Sangalang

Introduction

Welcome to Believe & Rise: The Power Of Your Story. My 5 Steps on how to create an empowering belief. My name is Emmanuel Sangalang. I am writing this book because I was once in your shoes. I had a goal I wanted to achieve but for some odd reason I could not do it. I did the research and found a lot of information. I read and saw testimonies on people achieving their goals. But why didn't I?

Have you ever had a goal that you have been talking about for years but for some reason you just never put in the time or effort to do it? That was me. I had a goal of leaving my full-time job to stay at home with my kids and build an online business that revolved around mindset coaching. I was not sure if this dream was even possible.

Here I am. It has been two years since I left my full-time job and I am enjoying every minute of it. I have learned so many things about my kids, my wife but most of all myself. I took that leap of faith and this is where I landed. I am writing this book and coaching regular people like you and me. The ones who have wondered, is this all there is to life? There has to be more. Or the ones that say, I know what I want but why can't I get there?

This all comes down to our limiting beliefs. Let's break those down and create empowering ones. Let us begin.

Pain. Struggle. Push. Pull. Inhale. Exhale!

The pain of feeling weak, the struggle of not being able to lift any more weight. Pushing through my limiting beliefs and pulling myself together with every inhale and exhale of each repetition.

I dropped the dumbbells and fell to the ground. I laid flat on the ground with my back against the rubber mats. Blinded by the fluorescent lights in the ceiling, I closed my eyes. Inhaled. Exhaled. I breathed heavily, and tried to catch my breath. Boom. Boom. My heart pounded as if it wanted to rip through my chest. Sweat dripped down my forehead and into my eyes. A burning sensation caused my eyes to shut tightly. Inhaled. Exhaled. Boom. Boom. I felt

Believe & Rise

weak. Destroyed. Defeated. A voice inside my head whispered, "*get up, stand up, breathe!*".

I turned to my right and I placed my hands on the ground and was on all fours. I heard beads of sweat drip down my face and splash on the rubber mats.

Inhaled. Exhaled. Boom. Boom.

I kneeled on one knee and opened my left eye. And my world began to slow down. I watched each bead of sweat slide off my face and splash on the mat.

Inhaled…Exhaled…Boom…Boom…

The voice repeated "*Get up. Stand up!*" I took a deep sigh and stood up. With both eyes open, I was now face to face with my greatest enemy! That one challenger that continued to knock me down! I walked towards him. I stared at him eye to eye, and saw the tremble in his eyes. I looked deeper into his eyes and focused on his pupils as though it were a tunnel to his soul. Finally with a stern voice I looked at my *reflection* and said, "Believe." Something shook inside of me, so I said it again. "Believe! Come on man! Believe!"

I closed my eyes, tilting my head down and I took a deep breath.

As I exhaled I opened my eyes and looked back up at my reflection.

I stared deep into my eyes, focusing only on my pupils, the tunnels to my soul, but now with confidence I said, "Rise!" I felt a jolt of energy as if a giant beast just woke up inside of me! I said it again! "Rise!" I clenched both my fist, stepped back and with a snarly voice I told myself, "Believe. And rise..." I nodded my head and felt the intensity build inside me. "Believe. And rise." Stronger! "Believe! And rise!" Louder! "Believe! And Rise!" Again! With power! "Believe! And Rise!" Come on! Right now! "Believe! And Rise! Believe! And Rise! Believe and Rise!

BELIEVE & RISE!!"....Boom….Boom.

My body began to tremble. I felt an intense energy flowing through me! As if I just broke the chains of a beast that's been tied down all these years! I closed my eyes and became one with the energy inside of me. I took a deep controlled breath and exhaled slowly. Opening my eyes I stepped forward and saw the new me! I nodded and said, "Yes! I see you! Welcome! I know who you are!

It's time to…

BELIEVE & RISE!!"

Emmanuel Sangalang

Chapter 1

Beware of your Labels

Growing up, I was called a bunch of names; Fat, Short, Dark, Dumb, Ugly, Filipino. We have all been called names before. But for me personally, there was one particular name that really stuck with me for a long time: *REPTILE*.

I know you are probably thinking, why would anyone call someone *"Reptile"*?

It was because of my skin. I have eczema. I have had it since I was a little kid. I have been able to control it more now, but I used to have really bad flare ups. Long story short, I was eight years old and I was at a dance practice with my cousins. One of the kids, who I just met, noticed my skin and said, "What's up with your skin? You look like a *Reptile*! Yeah I'm going to call you *Reptile*!" My cousins laughed and some would join in on his fun and call me *Reptile* as well. I didn't let it bother me too much but deep down. I hated that kid.

Later that night, I kept reliving that moment. That kid, calling me *Reptile* and my cousins who then joined him. All of them were pointing and laughing. I felt like I was watching a show on repeat. It was stuck in my head so I accepted the label.

Emmanuel Sangalang

> *A label is merely an opinion; it does not have to become your identity!*

Reminisce

Years have passed, and I've been approached with multiple opportunities to make income. The excitement with starting a business and working for myself also came with fear.. This is when one of my mentors introduced me to something called personal development. He told me to read books, watch videos, or listen to audio to help strengthen your mind.

I remember the first time I looked for a book to buy about Personal Development. My family and I were walking around the mall. I noticed a bookstore and I walked in, eager to look through all the Personal Development books. I walked up to the employee who was rearranging some books. With excitement I asked, "Can you direct me to the Personal Development section?" She gave me a look of confusion. I became disoriented. So I asked again. "Personal Development?" With uncertainty, she replied. "You mean Self Help?" Unsure with what she said, I just nodded. She then directed me to a small section in front of the cash register labelled *Self Help*. There were probably ten to fifteen books. I was shocked to see how small the section was. I shrugged my shoulders and grabbed the first book that caught my attention: "Take the Step, the Bridge will be there". This was the beginning of my personal development journey.

Over the years that followed, I religiously read, listened or watched something connected to personal development, self-help, and self-growth. I become aware of my thoughts and feelings. I began to ask myself questions; what am I afraid of? Why aren't I doing the steps necessary to build a business? Was there something that I needed to let go? What's holding me back? As I sat and pondered I unconsciously began to itch. Then it clicked. My skin? I am afraid that people will see my *Reptile* skin. I am afraid that people will judge me based on how my skin looks. They may feel disgusted and not want to talk to me.

I could not believe it. After all these years I am still holding on to this label. Why is that? Why am I still holding on to this label, it was only one day! Yes, it was only one day. But guess who kept saying it on the way home that night? Who said it before going to bed that night? Who said it the following morning? Who said it every time I got dressed? Who said it every time I began to itch? Who said it every time I looked in the mirror? Guess? It was **Me**.

There will be people out there that will place a label on you. They will try to define who you are. Do not let them. I encourage you to stop repeating that old label in your head. Stop living in the past.

Emmanuel Sangalang

> *"There's no such thing as a long time ago. There's only memories that mean something and memories that don't."*
> *-Sylvester Stallone*

Label Exercise

Take some time right now to write down a few labels that you have been holding on to. Ask yourself, whenever I am approaching a goal I'd like to accomplish, what do I connect "I can't because I am..." to? Think of your main 5 and write them down.

_____

_____

_____

_____

_____

Emmanuel Sangalang

I highly encourage you to take the time to write your top 5 down. Remember this is for you. If you don't write it down you will never know what your limiting beliefs are. Now go write them down. Stop reading and go. You will not be able to move forward without allowing these labels to surface. GO! Write them down.

Chapter 2

Definitions

I hope you did the exercise in the last chapter. I trust you did.

As a child I was raised in the Catholic way. There were rules to follow. You must behave while you are in church. Be quiet, no talking, no clapping, no dancing, and no laughing. Stand up, sit down, sing, praise and worship.

All these rules were fine. I really did not mind them. But something in the back of my mind would always question it. I would often see movies on TV that had people in the church clapping, dancing and laughing. Why don't we do that? The answer I usually heard was, we don't do that in our church. So I let it go.

I was a very curious kid. Just like *Curious George* always wondering why. As I dove deeper into personal development I could not help myself from wondering why. What are the reasons why we do the things we do? This led me to question my label.

After I realized my main label of *Reptile*. I could not help but wonder why this label was so effective in stopping me? And why was I still holding on to this label? I am obviously not a *Reptile*. So I asked myself, what does it mean to be a *Reptile*? What do I think of when I hear or even say the label *Reptile*? What do I tell myself?

I did not have a definite answer right away. I had to really think about it. I had to allow myself to relive the moment I first heard *Reptile*. It was uncomfortable thinking about that day. But the more I relived it, the easier it became for me to observe my thoughts.

After reliving my label a few times, I noticed that I was having an inner conversation with myself. Something we all know as our conscience. My conscience was telling me; *"You're a loser! You're ugly! No one likes you! You're gross! Stay away! Everyone's laughing at you! You're a joke!"*

This became the *definition* that I connected to the label *Reptile*. It meant that I was ugly. That I was scary looking. I was not welcome. I was disgusting. I was a monster. I was alone.

Emmanuel Sangalang

Words are just words until you connect an emotion to it. Then those words become memories.

Emotions

We are now aware of the label that has been holding us back. We also found the definition or meaning of the label that we have been repeating to ourselves. What's the next step? Emotions. These definitions, for now let's call them words, have an effect on us. These words create multiple feelings which I call *Emotional Triggers*.

As I began to pull back the layer of this label *Reptile* a story began to unfold. People laughing and people pointing. I am not welcome. I am ugly, disgusting. All these words connected to this one label. Now I asked myself, what am I feeling when I hear these words? How would I feel emotionally? My first response was that I felt sadness, pain, fear and anger.

- *Sadness*; this is the body I was given. I was born this way. I can't change it.

- *Pain*; this is my family. Family should not be treating family this way.

- *Fear*; if people are disgusted by me, who will want to be around me? Will I be alone?
- *Anger*; this kid has no right to talk to me this way. He doesn't even know me!

These were my *Emotional Triggers*. This is how I would feel whenever I was reminded of this old label. But this was just the beginning. If I did not get a grip of my emotions, I would spiral down a negative path that resulted in a life of no progress. I was never really the type to express my emotions. I would usually suppress what I was feeling and put on a smile. Pretending everything was fine.

We cannot change what we do not see.

Defining Our Labels

We have now brought to the surface our limiting beliefs; what I call our labels. The next step is to define these labels. Using the five labels that you wrote down I suggest that you pick a top three that you feel really impact you the most.

_____

_____

_____

Believe & Rise

    Now that you have decided on the three that impact you the most, it is time to choose one label that you believe really trembles your mind and soul. You know that deep down there is a deeper meaning behind this label. This label may have been placed on you from childhood, teenager hood, or even more recently.

_____

What meaning or definition are you associating with the label? I found the definition for my label by becoming aware of my conscience, the conversation in my head.

The definition/meaning that I am attaching to this label is:

_____

_____

_____

Emotional Triggers

We started with the label. We then listened to the inner conversation that we were having with ourselves. This next step requires us to combine it all and find the by-product of all these layers. What emotions are we feeling when this label appears? As you read from my experience, I felt *sadness, pain, fear* and *anger*. What do you feel?

When I hear or see this label I feel:

_____

_____

_____

Emmanuel Sangalang

I feel these emotional triggers because:

(Use my experience as a guide to your answer)

_____

_____

_____

Allow yourself to experience all emotional triggers that are coming up. This process can be a bit uncomfortable. That's okay. I have found that doing this brought me peace. This allowed me to feel alive again, allowing myself to just ride the wave of emotions that I had bottled up all this time.

Emotions and feelings are proof that you are living.

Chapter 3

Body Language

"A body at rest will remain at rest, and a body in motion will remain in motion unless it is acted upon by an external force."
-Newton's First Law of Motion

What does Newton's first law of motion have anything to do with *labels, definitions/meanings* and *emotional triggers*? Simple. Everything. The way we use our body affects the way we feel.

After I peeled back a few layers of my limiting beliefs, I felt great. I found the label I have been repeating all these years. I also defined what this label meant to me. I then connected these pieces to the emotional triggers that I was feeling. But for some odd reason I still felt down. I sat in my chair and wondered why? I wondered what I was missing. Then I read Newton's first law of motion, closed my eyes and imagined what I would do whenever I heard the label *Reptile*. Then it clicked. That's why I felt down. It was the way I was using my body. My body was in a downward motion. I slouched. My head was down. My body felt heavy. I wanted to hide. I wanted to cover up my body. Even the expression on my face was slightly downward. I would look down to avoid any eye contact.

Now if this is the motion that I have practiced through all these years, it will continue to stay in this motion. As stated in Newton's first law of motion. I have mastered these motions and now they have become an unconscious habit of mine.

Whenever I would hear the label *Reptile*, my conscience would kick. I would define what this label meant, and this would trigger my emotions. I would react to these emotions by positioning my body into a lower energy state. I would look down, I would look away, and I would feel discouraged. This became a default pattern. My truth.

Habits are built through the mastery of repetition.

Movement Exercise

We have arrived at what I believe is the final phase of becoming aware of our limiting beliefs. We brought to the surface our label, and listened to our conscience and the meaning/definition we gave our label. We then allowed ourselves to feel the emotions that we connected to this label. This is where we familiarize ourselves with the motion that our bodies have continued to move towards.

What motions are you making with your body after seeing or hearing your label? How is your posture? What is the expression on your face? How is your breathing?

Emmanuel Sangalang

_____

_____

_____

_____

We have completed the final exercise of becoming aware of our limiting beliefs. We found our label, gave it a meaning, felt the emotions, and now the way we move.

"For things to change, you have to change."
-Jim Rohn

Chapter 4

Breaking the Pattern

Before we move onto the next step, there is one final exercise we must do. See we took the necessary steps to become aware of our limiting beliefs. But what is going to happen if they show up again? We all know what that is like. We feel great, amazing, sometimes even motivated after immersing ourselves with all this information. This can happen after a seminar, audiobook, podcast, or networking event. Then we go home, excited to change, but the old patterns show up again. What do we do? Simple, we break the pattern.

We have all heard our favourite song play on the radio before. Yes, we all have different favourite songs, but there is always something about our own favourite song that makes us feel some type of way. Our favourite song can make us happy, sad, excited, pumped, and maybe even alive. We can listen to our favourite song hundreds of times and it will still have the same effect on us.

But let me ask you this; what happens if someone else creates their version of the song? Maybe a cover or even a remix. Does your favourite song now have the same impact? I don't think so. Sometimes the cover or remix can be even better than the original. Either way, our original thoughts towards our favourite song have now changed. What do I mean by all this?

There is a pattern that continues to unfold every time you hear or say your old label. Today we are going to interrupt, disturb, and possibly break that pattern so the effect is no longer the same. Just like making a cover or remix of our favourite song.

I am going to need full participation from you in this exercise.

Pattern Exercise

All you need are these three things. Music, Movement and Your Voice. Play a fun upbeat song that you have been listening to recently. Stand up and start dancing to it. Really feel the vibe of the music. Keep moving for the first minute of the song.

Now I want you to imagine a little whiny child when they don't get what they want. What is their body movement like and what does the sound of their voice sound like? I want you to impersonate the body language and sound of that child but I want you to say "I can't achieve my goals because I am (your label/limiting belief)!" I want you to say it out loud. Repeat this phrase at least five times. And after each time change your voice and your facial expressions. Remember to play full out, let loose and be silly!

1. First voice: "I can't achieve my goals because I am (Your Label)" Make a *Silly Face*!
2. Use a Different Voice: "I can't achieve my goals because I am (Your Label)" Make an *Angry Face*!
3. Use Another Voice: "I can't achieve my goals because I am (Your Label)" Make an *Overly Excited Face*!
4. Use a Crazy Voice: "I can't achieve my goals because I am (Your Label)" Make another *Silly Face*!
5. Now a Whiny Voice: "I can't achieve my goals because I am (Your Label) Make a *Surprised Face*!

This is an extremely fun exercise! I hope you enjoyed that. Doing this exercise will change how you feel about your limiting belief. Your limiting belief should sound and feel very different. If it does not. That means you did not fully commit to the exercise. So go do it again. Do this exercise as many times as you'd like. The more you disrupt your old pattern, the weaker it becomes. And if you really want to change you must commit to making this change!

Emmanuel Sangalang

Change is developed through repetition.

Chapter 5

What & Why?

When I was approached with multiple opportunities to replace my overnight job, I was too afraid to take action. After completing the exercises we just did, I was able to break down my limiting beliefs. I felt a sense of emptiness, like a blank canvas. This is the perfect opportunity to build a new empowering belief. This starts with *what & why*.

Becoming aware of my limiting beliefs was only half the battle. I had to figure out what I wanted and why I wanted to change. We have all heard it before, *"What's your why?"* We all have one. But let's start with *what*. What do I want?

What I wanted was to be at home with my family. I worked overnight shifts which really affected my health and mentality. Yes, I was home during the day but I was not present. I felt like a zombie treading around looking for some source of energy to keep me up right.

Without being clear in what I wanted I would never figure out a direction to go. Imagine looking at a map and just staring at it. If you have not made a decision on where you want to go, that map is nothing more than just an image. We must make that decision first in order to move towards that goal.

What is that goal you are wanting to achieve?

_____

_____

_____

_____

Emmanuel Sangalang

> *You will only get what you want in life when you have decided what that is.*

Why?

Figuring out our *why* is also important for achieving our goals. Our *why* provides a spark to our *what*. As I said earlier, we all have a *why*. Now we must ask ourselves; is my *why* compelling enough? Does your '*why*' get you up out of bed? Will your '*why*' stand firmly against the naysayers? It is one thing to have a *why* but it is another thing to have a *why* that really moves you. In order for me to have a compelling enough *why,* I had to figure out my "*why not*". That's right, *why not*. If I don't change what will happen? What will my inaction result in?

This part may be a bit confusing, but the answer I have found for my *why not* was to ask more questions. Questions like: Am I okay with living the way I have? Am I okay not going after my dreams? Am I okay knowing that I chose not to make that sacrifice for my kids? Am I okay with missing out on the memories of my children growing up? Am I okay not being present?

Emmanuel Sangalang

> *This present time is God's gift to you.*

Finding out my *why not* will only enhance my *why*. This process was very emotional. I had to take the time to really visualize what I wanted and why I wanted to achieve it. Then I had to visualize what would happen if I didn't. I created such a painful '*why not*' that it brought me to tears.

There are three categories of life that are very important to all of us. Health, wealth and relationships. These categories will help build up your *why* and *why not*.

My Initial *Why Not*:

I will continue to live a life of regret. I will also miss out on moments with my children that I can never get back. My children are constantly growing and experiencing life and if I don't change I will never be there.

My *Why Not* with the three categories:

- **Health:** How will my *health* be affected if I don't achieve my goal?
- I will continue to gain weight. My arthritis will take over my life.
- **Wealth:** How will my *wealth* be affected if I don't achieve my goal?
- My income will stay the same. I have reached the top of the salary that I can make working this job. I will be stuck. No growth.
- **Relationships:** How will my *relationships* be affected if I don't achieve my goal?
- I will continue to miss out on moments that I cannot get back. I will not be present with my kids or my wife. My relationships will fall apart.

This was not a fun process. This brought me into a very negative state. But now that I have pulled myself into this low energy this means I must catapult myself into a higher, beautiful state. I do this by asking new empowering questions with the three categories.

The arrow can only hit its target when firs pulled back.

My Why with the three categories:

- **Health:** How will my *health* change once I achieve my goal?

- I will have more freedom to focus on my health. I will be able to enjoy eating instead of emotionally eating. My arthritis is gone. I will be able to play sports again.
- **Wealth:** How will my *wealth* change once I achieve my goal?

- I will have no limit to any amount of income I want to receive. Money flows through me in abundance.
- **Relationships:** How will my *relationships* change once I achieve my goal? -   I will create new memories with my family filled with laughter. I am present.
Nothing else is true. Just the moments that I am currently enjoying with them. I am empowered by my relationships and they feed off of my energy.

As you can see. Our *why* is not that simple to answer. I had to pull myself into a negative space so I can catapult into a compelling future. My *why* excites me. It fills my soul. It allows me to enjoy what I am doing.

Take as much time as you need for the next exercise. I want you to play full out. Take breaks and make sure you breathe while you figure out your *why not* & *why*. I realized that I knew more of what my *why not* was because I was already living it. But my *why not* really affected me when I imagined if my future was still the same. If nothing changed. If I fast forwarded five years from now and I still did not achieve my goal. How would I really feel? Would I be okay with that?

Be truly honest with yourself in this process. The truth will actually set you free. It will set you free from all your old limiting beliefs and allow you to build up a strong foundation for your new empowering beliefs.

Emmanuel Sangalang

Exercise: Why Not?

_____

_____

_____

_____

Believe & Rise

3 Categories (Why Not)

Health: How will my health be affected if I don't achieve my goal?

_____

_____

_____

_____

Wealth: How will my wealth be affected if I don't achieve my goal?

_____

_____

Believe & Rise

Relationship: How will my relationships be affected if I don't achieve my goal?

_____

_____

_____

You may start to feel that same low energy that I was experiencing. That's okay. But understand that you do not have to stay there. You can change and you will. But that change can only happen once you have made that decision to change. So make that shift right now. Ask yourself uplifting questions. Answer with confidence and certainty. Answer as if you have already achieved your goals. Answer like you have accomplished every goal you have set with ease and determination. Let's do this.

Believe & Rise

3 Categories (Why)

Health: How has my health changed now that I have accomplished my goal?

_____

_____

_____

_____

Wealth: How has my wealth changed now that I have accomplished my goal?

_____

_____

_____

_____

_____

Believe & Rise

Relationships: How have my relationships changed now that I have achieved my goal?

_____

_____

_____

_____

Summarize your answers from 3 Categories (Why) into a few statements. This will become your *why*.

Emmanuel Sangalang

My Why:

_____

_____

    Your *what* and *why* is the beginning of the creation for your new empowering beliefs. You have just set the foundation. It is time to build on this and continue to **Believe & Rise**!

Chapter 6

Power Stance

The Superman stance. Stand up, place your hands on your hips, feet shoulder width apart, chest up, chin up and look forward with confidence. Control your breathing. Simply do this for at least two minutes and scientifically your body will begin to produce more testosterone. A natural increase of testosterone in the body will improve your mood. So what does this have to do with your new empowering belief? This power stance shows us that our mood can change simply by changing the way we position our body.

Remember in Chapter 3 when I shared with you how my body was every time I would hear or see the label of *Reptile*? Well this time we are using that same method, Newton's First Law of Motion, to build on our new empowering belief. We are building momentum so we can continue to stay in this beautiful state. I used this process to build my Power Move. I slap my chest, clench both my fists and yell "Ahhh!"

Deep down I believe that we all have a Power Stance or Power Move inside of us. We just have to find it. There are many ways of figuring out your Power Move, but the method I found very effective was sports. I was very active growing up. I played Basketball, Volleyball, Tennis, Soccer, and even competed in Dance. There's something all of these sports have in common, scoring a point or just winning in general. There is a move that most athletes do when they have achieved something. We have all seen it before. That clenched fist thrown or pumped in some type of direction accompanied with the phrase "YES!".

Try this simple gesture; clench your first really tight and say "Yes". Say it again but louder. "YES!" Again but with more emotion.

Believe & Rise

"YES!" One more time, but imagine you've already achieved your goal. Say it! "YES!"

You may begin to feel some type of adrenaline fill your body. This is just the beginning. Next I would like for you to imagine a superhero, or someone you idolize. How does this person stand? Do they have a specific body gesture that sticks out to you?

Spider-man when he launches his web, Superman when stands strong, athletes like LeBron James when he throws the powder in the air, Steph Curry as he points to the sky. We all have some type of body gesture that we unconsciously do when we have completed a task or achieved a goal. Find yours. If you can't find yours right at this moment use someone else's. Eventually yours will show up.

Your Power Move

Are you creating your own Power move or will you be using a Superhero, Athlete, or someone you idolize?

_____

Describe your Power Move. What are you doing with your body? How are you using your voice?

_____

_____

_____

Believe & Rise

Chapter 7

Exciting Emotions

After I created my Power Move, I noticed that I felt different. I knew I had to ask myself what exciting emotion has this move produced for me? My automatic answers were strong, powerful, brave and confident. You will see that there is now a story that is being structured as you continue down this path to creating your empowering belief.

While we go through this chapter, imagine your power move. Mentally do it and experience the emotions that you are feeling each time you do it. Each time you take it up one notch producing an even higher power. Demand more of yourself and create more certainty. Being in this state will bring you closer and closer to achieving your goal. Allow the emotions to flow through every part of your body. From the top of your head to the bottom of your feet. Feel the tingly sensation in your hands each time you move them. Breathe deep. Each inhale is absorbing every emotion that you are feeling. Let the emotions fuel your mind, body and spirit. Exhale as reassurance that you have accepted this new you. Close your eyes and listen to the voice that is in your head. Breathe.

Open your eyes. Stay in this energy and share your experience. You must write everything that you are feeling down onto paper. Doing this will remind yourself of the power that you can produce from within. You have always had this ability but now you must take control. Use the information that you will write on paper as a resource to your power move.

New abilities lead to new achievements.

Express the Energy

What are you feeling now that you have created a Power move for yourself? State some of the emotions that you are feeling.

_____

_____

_____

_____

_____

Chapter 8

Permission

A new energy has just filled our entire being. I feel different. I feel better. Now that I feel this way, I am no longer afraid to go after my goals. I am focusing on what I feel and I am going towards my goal. Because of all these exciting emotions I have given myself the permission to move in the right direction.

Now that I have given myself that permission I did what I was too afraid to do. For me, that thing I was afraid of was starting a conversation with people. Inviting people to the opportunity that I have. Saying yes to myself. Sharing with strangers my journey. Finding a mentor. Mindset coaching individuals like you and I. Start writing this book. Finish writing this book.

These were all the tasks that I believed that I was not good enough to achieve. I was afraid that people would see my *Reptile* skin. All of these tasks were compiled by the amount of information that I dove into at the beginning of my journey. I needed to find out HOW can I achieve my goals? I stored all this valuable information into the back of my mind. Mainly because I would always be triggered by my old label. You have an abundance of information stored in the back of your mind as well. All those YouTube videos you watched, the podcasts and Audible you listened to. Even the one on one coaching that you have experienced. You have a collection waiting to be put to use. Well guess what? Now is the time to use it. Give yourself that permission to use all of your valuable information and implement them today.

The permission is yours.

Implementation Exercise

Information has power. But without execution and implementation it is more like a burden. We all know what it is like to want to achieve a goal. We would dive into all the "how to's" of achieving it. We can all find the information on how to do something but none of us will truly understand what that is like unless we go and experience it. Now you do not need to go find more information. Use what you already have. You have all the information you need sitting in the back of your mind.

Just decide what the information is and give yourself permission to use it.

What will you be implementing now that has once scared you in the past? This is usually connected to the statement, "I know how to do that but...." From this point on you will now say, "I will!" I will go make the cold call. I will start my fitness program today. I will start my business today.
I will:

_____

Chapter 9

Identity

Embarking on this journey of creating an empowering belief has shifted me in a way that is hard to explain. I truly have changed. Better yet, I have evolved. I have not changed who I am, but I have become a better, stronger, more confident version of myself.

We have unveiled our old limiting belief, removed that label, rearranged the meaning and emotional triggers the label gave us. We then began the process of building an empowering belief. Starting with a blank canvas we produced a power move which led to exciting emotions. Giving ourselves the permission to push forward and now here we are. Let us seal this entire package up with an identity.

I knew that if I am going to achieve my goals, I needed to look at myself in a different way. I had to evolve from the inside out. Setting these new practices and doing them on a regular basis created a new version of myself. I stare at my reflection now with pride, confidence, power, joy, laughter, happiness. I am a *Warrior*. Nothing can stop me from achieving my goals. I am in charge. I am proud of who I am becoming. I will continue to grow and inspire others to do the same. I am a *Warrior*. I will never give up when times get tough. I will get up as many times as I need to so nothing is holding me back. I am a *Warrior*. I will fight for my dreams because my family deserves the best of me. I deserve the best of myself! I am a *Warrior*!

Emmanuel Sangalang

> *Your identity is the standard that you set for yourself.*

New Identity

We must set a higher standard for ourselves. Only the great achievers in life do this and you are one of them. I knew that you would be able to achieve your goals once you started reading this book. That is because I will always believe in you. Now it is time for you to believe in yourself. You have completed all the exercises from above. Now seal this new version of you with your new identity. So I ask you this, **who are you?**

I AM

_____!

You have created such a powerful identity. Now you must go back to the previous chapters and create some empowering statements that can support your identity. Your power move, the exciting emotions you felt, the permission you have given yourself. Prior to reading this book, you had a goal that you wanted to achieve. But your old limiting belief was holding you back. Let us do the last exercise and create your empowering belief.

Emmanuel Sangalang

I am a WARRIOR.

Chapter 10

Empowering Belief

We have reached the very last exercise of this book. This is where you will embody everything we have discussed in this book. The first time I did this exercise I was alone in the bathroom. So I highly encourage you to do this alone in your room or bathroom somewhere that has a mirror. If there are people in the house, warn them that you will get loud. If there's no one home perfect.

Things you will need:

- Music (Upbeat or Instrumental workout music)
- Mirror (One you do not need to hold)
- Your Power Move
- Your New Identity

Before we get into the exercise I would like for you to write this statement down:

"I can, I will, I must because I am (*Your New Identity*)! **Believe & Rise!**"

Now that you have written this down, go into the room where you will be doing this exercise. Repeat the line you just wrote multiple times in your head. Memorize it. Say it out loud a few times. When you are ready, play the music. Take three deep breaths. Inhale, exhale. Close your eyes and allow your body to feel the music. Take another three deep breaths then open your eyes. Now stare at your reflection. Focus only on your pupils. Nothing else matters in this moment, just you.

Mirror Exercise

Inhale. Exhale. Now do your move and say the statement:

"I can. I will. I must because I am (*Your New Identity*)!
Believe & Rise!"

Breathe. Do your move again and now go louder!

"I can. I will. I must because I am (*Your New Identity*)!
Believe & Rise!"

Again. Now with more POWER!

"I can. I will. I must because I am (*Your New Identity*)!
Believe & Rise!"

Last time! All you got! Do your move! Say it loud!

"I can. I will. I must because I am (*Your New Identity*)!
Believe & Rise!"

Breathe. Inhale Exhale. Stare at your reflection again. Breathe. Focusing only on your pupils, the tunnels to your soul. Feel the tingles in your hands and body. Feel the energy inside you begin to rise. Breathe. Keep staring. Now say:

"Yes! Here I am! Yes! Welcome the New Me! *Believe & Rise!"*

Congratulations

Congratulations on discovering your new empowering belief. I have given you the tools that have helped me break free from my own limiting beliefs. I continue to produce new empowering beliefs using this exact method. I have not shown you anything new. You have heard all of this before. Everything that you have produced came from within you. You are capable of anything. You must believe that!

Thank you so much for taking the time to read this book. If you feel like this book has helped you or may help someone you know. Feel free to send them a copy.

GIVEAWAY
Experience the *Mirror Exercise* with me at:

www.BelieveAndRise.ca

Until next time. Remember there is no greater time than right now. It's time to…

Emmanuel Sangalang

BELIEVE
&
RISE!

Up next…

Believe & Rise

The Power of Your Surroundings.

Emmanuel Sangalang

Manufactured by Amazon.ca
Bolton, ON